TAKE ACTION WITH ANIMALS!

ANIMALS UNDER THE SEA

Written by
Madeline Tyler

Illustrated by
Amy Li

WINDMILL BOOKS

Published in 2022 by Windmill Books,
an Imprint of Rosen Publishing
29 East 21st Street, New York, NY 10010

© 2020 Booklife Publishing
This edition is published by arrangement with Booklife Publishing

All rights reserved. No part of this book may be reproduced in any form without permission in writing from the publisher, except by a reviewer.

Edited by: John Wood
Illustrated by: Amy Li

Cataloging-in-Publication Data
Names: Tyler, Madeline. | Li, Amy.
Title: Animals under the sea / by Madeline Tyler, illustrated by Amy Li.
Description: New York : Windmill Books, 2022. | Series: Take action with animals!
Identifiers: ISBN 9781499487503 (pbk.) | ISBN 9781499487527 (library bound) |
ISBN 9781499487510 (6 pack) | ISBN 9781499487534 (ebook)
Subjects: LCSH: Marine animals--Juvenile fiction.
Classification: LCC PZ7.1.T954 An 2022 | DDC [E]--dc23

Printed in the United States of America

CPSIA Compliance Information: Batch CSWM22: For Further Information contact Rosen Publishing, New York, New York at 1-800-237-9932

Find us on

All images courtesy of Shutterstock. With thanks to Getty Images, Thinkstock Photo, and iStockphoto.
Cover – KateChe, malven57, Toluk, flovie, Anna Timoshenko. Recurring backgrounds – malven57, begun1983, Only background. Recurring texture brushes – Toluk (grunge), flovie (spotty), Anna Timoshenko (rock cracks), Tartila (plant elements). 2–3 – ag1100, 8–11 – abeadev, freelanceartist, Golden Shrimp, MiraElArt, New Line, Nelosa, 12–15 – Grunge Creator, 16–19 – Curly Pa, 20–23 – Curly Pa, Miloje, SeamlessPattern.

Can you use your imagination to take a trip to the bottom of the sea?

Follow the **INSTRUCTIONS** on each page and see what you can find.

Who is hiding in this shell?

Tell them that it is time for breakfast.

Say
"BREAKFAST!"
and turn the page...

It is a hungry
sea turtle!

This is a **puffer fish**.

What happens if you **BLOW** on the puffer fish?

WOW!

Look at it now!

Can you see the stingray underneath the sand?

Try **SHAKING** the book and turning the page...

13

Octopuses have eight arms.

TICKLE

the octopus and turn the page...

Oh no!

There is ink everywhere!

Who is hiding in the dark?

TAP

the fish to turn on the light...

It is an

anglerfish!

Can you match each animal to its home?